DESIGN**TOPICS**

Design in Society

Terry Liddament

Oxford University Press

INTRODUCTION

The history of design is in large part the history of the everyday artefacts which surround us in our daily lives. To understand these artefacts properly we need to see them in their social and historical context. This book introduces students to some of the main elements which shape this context. It considers influences from the past, material resources, the development of manufacturing techniques, changing needs, marketing, advertising, and retailing, as well as the growth of urbanisation, the visual environment, transport, industry, and leisure.

In becoming more aware of these influences it is hoped that students will not only be able to take a greater pleasure in looking at artefacts both past and present, but will also be better able to make informed choices, both as consumers, and as citizens in an increasingly complex world.

Terry Liddament 1991

Oxford University Press, Walton Street, Oxford OX2 6DP

Oxford   New York   Toronto
Delhi   Bombay   Calcutta   Madras   Karachi
Petaling Jaya   Singapore   Hong Kong   Tokyo
Nairobi   Dar es Salaam   Cape Town
Melbourne   Auckland

and associated companies in
Berlin   Ibadan

Oxford is a trade mark of Oxford University Press

© Terry Liddament

First published 1991 , reprinted 1992

A CIP catalogue record for this book is available from the British Library.

ISBN 0 19 832779 X

Typeset in News Gothic by
Tradespools Ltd, Frome, Somerset
Printed in France by Pollina, 85400 Luçon - n° 15020

Acknowledgements

Anglepoise p 57 (left); **Architectural Association/V Bennett** pp 41 (bottom right), **/Alan Chandler** 41 (bottom centre), **/Julian Freary** 41 (centre right), **/Gale Tattersall** 42 (top), **/Hazel Cook** 43 (top), **/Hubert Bennett** 44 (top); **Barnabys Photographic Library** pp 6, 26, 39, 47 (bottom right), 58 (bottom right), 59; **Bournville Village Trust** p 42 (bottom); **British Museum** p 9 (bottom right); **British Rail** pp 14 (top), 50 (bottom left); **British Telecom** p 11; **Britvic Soft Drinks** p 35 (left); **Brookes & Adams** p 24 (bottom); **J Allan Cash** pp 44 (centre right), 47 (bottom right), 60 (centre right); **Casio Electronics** p 38 (top); **Consumers' Association** p 53 (bottom left & right); **Fiona Corbridge** p 55 (top & bottom right); **Electricity Council** p 35 (top right); **Mary Evans Picture Library** pp 17 (centre right), 18 (top), 23 (bottom), 40 (top); **Ford Motor Company** pp 21 (left & bottom right), 51 (top); **Steven Garner** p 46; **Sally & Richard Greenhill** pp 15 (bottom), 51 (centre), 58 (centre right); **Ron Herron** p 50 (centre); **Hille** p 57 (top right); **Hoover** p 27 (centre); **Hulton Picture Company** pp 16 (top), 17 (top right), 20 (top), 40 (left), 41 (top right), 43 (right), 49 (top left), 52 (top right), 53 (centre right); **Ikea** pp 38 (bottom, 51 (bottom); **Imperial War Museum** p 53 (top right); **Kays** p 7 (bottom); **Last Resort** p 39; **London Transport Museum** p 37 (top & centre right); **Manchester City Art Galleries** p 18 (bottom); **Millets Leisure** p 58 (top right); **Musei Civici, Como** p 50 (top); **National Motor Museum** pp 26 (top right), 57 (centre right); **National Museum of Photography, Film & Television** p 33 (top left); **Popperfoto** pp 30 (top), 56 (top left & right); **Porsche** p 13 (bottom); **Renault** p 13; **Royal Pavilion, Art Gallery & Museums, Brighton** p 6 (centre); **Russell Hobbs** pp 4 (bottom), 27 (top), 58 (left); **Science Museum, London** pp 4, 8, 20, 21, 30, 31; **Sony UK Ltd** p 13; **South Yorkshire Police** p50 (bottom right); **Spectrum** pp 14 (bottom right), 15 (centre right), 39 (left), 59 (top right); **Stannah Lifts** p 54 (top); **P M Straker Welds** p 12; **Victoria & Albert Museum** pp 9, 10, 19 (right); **Elizabeth Whiting** p 52 (bottom left); **Wrangler** p 35 (bottom right); **Zefa Photographic Library** pp 14 (centre right), 27 (bottom right), 45 (right), 46 (right), 49 (left), 55 (left).

Additional photography by **Chris Honeywell** and **Terry Liddament**.

Oxford University Press would like to thank the following for their kind help and assistance: **Barclays Bank plc, Lewis's plc** and **Gerry Wells** from the Vintage Wireless Museum.

Illustrations by **Colin Elgie, JonesSewell** and **Julie Tolliday**.

CONTENTS

Design in the past

Most of the things we use in our everyday lives have been designed by someone – from houses, furniture, and clothes, to personal stereos and toothbrushes. We seldom stop to think how they were made, or how they came to look as they do, or what the reasons are for their existence. Yet the story of their development from earlier times is often fascinating, and we can deepen our understanding of their design by studying the way they have developed from the past.

Understanding the past can help us to understand the present. Think for a moment of your own past. If you wanted to tell someone about yourself you would probably refer to things that had happened to you, things you had done, and so on. Telling them things like that would be a way of explaining what kind of person you are. You would, of course, need to rely on your memory. Even if you kept a diary, and could use it to help, you would still need to remember that you had written the diary!

Without memory, you would have no knowledge of your own past, and you would find it difficult to explain the kind of person you are. A society with no knowledge of its past might be in much the same position. Society needs some knowledge of the past in order to understand the present.

Everyday objects change through time

Changes in design and technology affect the way people live

Historians study the past in an organized and systematic way. They can perform a valuable task in helping to provide society with a proper sense of its past. We can learn a lot about the way people lived by studying the things they used – and studying the changes in those objects can help us to appreciate present-day design.

The past around us

A significant part of the past is still very much with us. A walk down any street in any town will reveal this. Many houses and other buildings have survived from the past. Some in your town may even be several hundreds of years old. The important ones may have been preserved as museums or other places of interest. You can visit these in order to learn about the past.

Many older buildings in the town or city where you live will have an interesting past. A Victorian workhouse may have been converted into flats, or an old church may now be used as a community centre. Looking at these buildings can often give clues about their past.

Buildings from Tudor times in Elm Hill, Norwich

ASSIGNMENTS

● Find out from older members of your family or community how everyday living has changed since they were young. Make a record of the changes they mention.

● Look through family photograph albums and make notes of any changes in the way people dress, hairstyles, and so on.

● Look around the area in which you live, making notes and sketches of different kinds of houses, their appearance, and the materials they are built with. Try to find out when they were built.

The past around us 2

Buildings are by no means the only things to have survived from the past. Objects of many different kinds are preserved in museums so that we may all appreciate them. Some of these are quite valuable, or unique. But there are also countless ordinary, everyday objects around us which can tell us much of interest when we study them carefully. Many of these will be found in our own homes. You may have some items in your home which have belonged to your family for a long time.

These objects are **artefacts** – that is, they have all been designed and made by somebody at some time or other. Studying them can tell us a good deal about the people who made them, the people who used them, the reasons for the artefacts coming into existence, and why they took the particular form that they did.

Pair of matching vases, 1920s

QUESTIONS

● Look at the photographs of everyday objects on these two pages. Do you have any of these objects at home? Some are now valuable collector's items.

● What can these artefacts tell us about the past? Compare them to modern versions of the same things, and think about the reasons for the differences between them.

Platform shoes, 1970s

Borrowing from the past

Studying buildings, houses, furniture, clothing, and other artefacts from the past is an important part of studying design in society. By looking closely at them you can get a better understanding of much present-day design. The appearance, form, and function of many present-day artefacts are derived from the past. When you examine artefacts closely you will see that designers have often been guided by the appearance of artefacts from earlier times. They have used ideas about the way artefacts should look which are borrowed from the past.

This building was designed and erected in the middle of the nineteenth century, but it is dressed up in the style of a medieval castle, complete with turrets and battlements. This style is called **Gothic**. Many buildings were built to look like this during the nineteenth century, when the medieval period was much admired.

Harpur Centre, Bedford

This clock is modern, and has a quartz movement based on the latest ideas in the technology of timekeeping. But the clock has a pendulum which actually swings, to make it look like a pendulum clock of much earlier design. Here, the designer has borrowed the design from a style of clock which was popular in the eighteenth century.

QUESTIONS

● Make a collection of some other everyday objects which borrow from the past in this way. Why do you think they have been made to look like that?

Tradition and invention

Oldsmobile, 1904

Heal's radio cabinet, 1924

Magnet cooker, 1924

Designers may have several reasons for wishing to borrow from the past. The building and the clock shown on page 7 were made to look like artefacts from periods of the more distant past because the styles of those periods have been very much admired in more recent times. Nostalgia – the yearning for a vanished past – may also explain the popularity of older designs.

But new inventions can present designers with a challenge. The first motor cars looked rather like horse-drawn carriages. Designers, and the people who bought these early machines, perhaps felt more secure with familiar forms.

Designers may find it difficult to break away from established ideas about the way things should look, or they may sometimes feel that the public is not ready for radical change. Another problem for designers is that they may lack the materials and techniques which would make it possible to create new designs.

The design of this early American motor car clearly derives from the horse-drawn carriages it was seeking to replace. The people who made it could draw upon traditional carriage-making skills to a great extent, and its appearance would have reassured a suspicious public.

When radio was first used, designers had the task of housing the components inside a suitable cabinet. This wireless set was made in 1924. When the doors were closed it looked just like an ordinary piece of furniture.

Early electric cookers were another example of reliance on familiar forms. This 1924 cooker is more like a traditional solid-fuel stove than an electrical appliance.

QUESTIONS

● What reasons can you suggest for the appearance of the wireless and the cooker?

Form and function

Some designers, while retaining respect for the past, rejected the copying of past styles. Instead, they tried to create forms for familiar artefacts which, although drawing on the past to some extent, aimed at introducing new ideas.

The two chairs shown here illustrate this difference in approach clearly. One is of a fairly typical design of the 1870s. It is rather elaborate and heavily upholstered. The other chair is from the same period, but here the designer has tried to create a clear and uncluttered form.

There is also a marked contrast in the designs of the two teapots shown here, which are also from the same period. One is elaborately decorated with lots of ornamental detail, while the other is a simple design with no added decoration.

William Morris, who designed the simple, rush-seated chair above, and Christopher Dresser, the designer of the box-like teapot, both believed that the appearance of an artefact should clearly show its function or purpose. They insisted that everyday items should have a clear, straightforward construction and be honestly made, with no unnecessary decoration. They both belonged to a group of designers which became known as the **Arts and Crafts Movement**, which was formed by Morris in 1883.

The Arts and Crafts designers turned against what they saw as the overdecorated, muddled, and dishonest style of much nineteenth-century design. They blamed the industrial methods of production which were replacing the more traditional methods of handcraftsmanship during this period. They argued that manufacturers needed the expertise of trained designers to guide them in producing good designs for the new methods of industrial production.

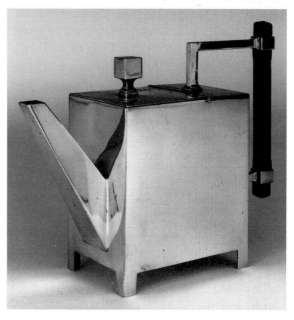

QUESTIONS

● The rush-seated chair shown above is still a very popular design. Study the chair carefully, and then give reasons which might explain this popularity.

Design for machine production

The designers of the Arts and Crafts Movement had a strong influence on design. Many of their ideas are still influential. The view that an artefact's form should be dictated by its function, and that it should be fitted for its purpose, has guided many designers since.

Arts and Crafts designers, however, were criticized during the early years of the twentieth century. Their critics accused them of failing to come to terms with the challenge of designing artefacts that could be mass produced on machines.

This challenge, as some saw it, was to create designs that were fully adapted to manufacture by machines, instead of the handcraftsmanship that the Arts and Crafts designers relied on. This was an important point, because it was only through the use of machines that production could be speeded up, and costs brought down. Lower costs for goods would mean that more people could afford them.

Designers were also seeking to establish a style that would clearly express the new age of the machine, which they felt was dawning at the beginning of the twentieth century.

The stainless steel chair shown here had a very 'modern' appearance when it was first made. It was designed by Marcel Breuer, who firmly believed that everyday items of domestic furniture should clearly express the new materials and technology of the twentieth century.

The plywood chair shown here was designed by Gerald Summers. It also shows how designers in the early twentieth century were seeking functional yet elegant forms which could be produced using machinery.

Wardrobe by the Arts and Crafts designer Edward Barnsley, 1902

QUESTIONS

● Look at the two illustrations of chairs on this page. What features do they have that made them suitable for manufacture by machines?

Design: a visual vocabulary

The artefacts that survive from the past are our raw material, so to speak. As you study them more closely, you can 'read off' many interesting things about them. Learning how to look is an important part of this process. This is rather like learning a language. All designers rely to some extent on a kind of 'visual vocabulary'. You can learn to read this vocabulary with a little practice.

As you have noticed, there are several influences at work on the designers' vocabulary. For one thing, it is often influenced by the past. But it also changes through time as new ideas about the way things should look are introduced.

In addition, new technology often has an important influence on designers. It has frequently challenged them to create suitable forms for entirely new artefacts. It has also forced them to rethink the design of these artefacts as technological knowledge and skills have developed.

The telephone, now familiar in our daily lives, is an example of how all these things can come to have some influence on the appearance of an artefact. Telephones have changed quite markedly since their first appearance. New materials such as plastics have been developed, and the mechanism has been refined through improvements in manufacturing techniques. Telephones have also become lighter, more portable and easier to use, as well as being more consciously styled to blend in with the home, the office, or even the motor car.

Early telephone handset

Telephone handset, 1960s

Telephones today

QUESTIONS

● What are the main changes in appearance of the telephones here?

● Which of these changes would you say are due to technology?

● What other influences might there have been?

ASSIGNMENTS

● When you are out shopping for personal items such as clothes, make a careful note of the kinds of thing which influence your choices. If you are with friends, try to get their opinions.

Artefacts tell stories

As you can see, the designer's visual vocabulary changes through time. You can appreciate some of these changes by studying the changing appearances of artefacts. Here is a radio set, designed and made in 1934, together with some ideas which can help you get a better understanding of the visual vocabulary that the designer used.

EKCO radio, 1934

What is its appearance?

The designer has gone for a bold, cylindrical form which is taken up and echoed by all the parts of the radio cabinet. The only departure from this is the use of vertical struts in the speaker grille. The surface is smooth and dark, and helps to make the sweep of the dial stand out clearly.

What was its purpose?

It was intended as a radio receiver. But notice how the designer has set about expressing the then new technology of radio by using a bold, futuristic looking form. It is interesting to contrast this with the radio cabinet on page 8, which sticks instead to a traditional furniture form.

Whom was it intended for?

The British Broadcasting Corporation, which was the only radio broadcasting organization at the time, had a potentially immense audience by the 1930s. Manufacturers were beginning to realize the commercial possibilities. This design aimed at impressing the wonders and benefits of the new technology on the public.

How was it made?

The designer used a material called Bakelite, which was an early form of **plastic**. Bakelite could be moulded in a press. It was this material that helped the designer to break away from the older, wooden furniture forms, and create a new and more exciting image in keeping with the technology of radio.

The radio was made by a company called EKCO, and the designer was Wells Coates. His achievement here was to help create a new visual vocabulary for a new technology. Other manufacturers gradually began to follow this example.

QUESTIONS

● List the things you notice about the visual vocabulary of the design of the Porsche shown here.

Evolution in design

You have been looking at artefacts from the past. Studying these can also help us understand their present-day descendants.

The radios shown here are all distant relatives of the EKCO radio shown opposite. One of the most important changes is in the size of their components. Radio technology has developed considerably since the 1930s to produce much smaller parts. The circuits and speaker components can now be miniaturized, resulting in really portable products.

Changing needs

People's needs have also changed. Most homes now have several radios, each used in a different way to fulfil a different kind of need. So too have people's attitudes. The radio is now accepted as a more workaday artefact alongside the many other items in the average home.

Yet people are still captivated by the power and glamour of radio as a device for bringing the world 'out there' directly to them. This feature is a part of people's attitude towards radio which you can also see reflected in the forms which designers create – forms which symbolize this power.

The present-day motor car is also a development from earlier designs. As with radio, motor technology has improved, resulting in greater efficiency, economy, and safety. Plastics and aluminium alloys have cut down on weight, while improvements in engine design have led to better performance from smaller engines.

Again, people's needs have changed, resulting in a greater variety of vehicles, ranging from the everyday family runabout to the high-performance luxury sports car. It is interesting to see how often manufacturers try to combine these different qualities in one vehicle. But, as with radio, the glamour and excitement of the motor car still tend to survive from earlier times. Fantasy is still an ingredient in their design.

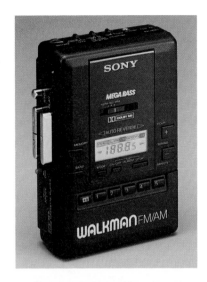

QUESTIONS

● Make a list of the different needs the artefacts shown here fulfil.

● What kinds of attitude do you see reflected in their appearance?

Designing today

Design in our society has become increasingly important as society's demands have grown more complex. Designers, in response to these demands, have become more professional, and designing has become a career in its own right. Many of the artefacts created by designers are for our personal use – clothes, domestic goods, and so on. However, design is not only concerned with personal possessions.

Transport systems such as the rail network employ skilled designers to work on a wide range of design problems. These include the design and layout of seating on trains, the styling and livery of the carriages and locomotives, and even the public information signs.

Space travel is only possible through the efforts of a large team of experts. Some of them are designers who will work on design problems like the layout of instruments and control systems in spacecraft, the design of food packaging systems for use in space, and so on.

We are all designers

Yet design is by no means an area reserved for professional designers. We are all involved in designing to some extent, and probably more than we realize.

When we buy clothes, or items for our homes, we are making choices about our appearance and our surroundings. These are design decisions, and when we make these choices, we are involved in designing our appearance, or our surroundings. The choices we make can have an influence on designers, and hence on design.

Inter-City 225 **high speed train**

Design in the home

QUESTIONS

● Make a list of your favourite clothes and music. Give reasons for your choices.

● Compare your list with a friend's list. Give reasons for your agreements and also your disagreements.

Progress in design

Progress in design can be thought of in a number of ways – for example, as discoveries and developments in science and technology. Or it can be thought of as improvements in the quality of the environment we live in, or perhaps as changes in fashion and style, clothes and music.

One way of measuring progress might be to record important changes. For example, in rail transport:

■ Richard Trevithick built the first steam train in 1804;

■ George Stephenson built his first locomotive, *Blucher*, in 1814;

■ the Liverpool and Manchester Railway opened in 1830, powered by Stephenson's *Rocket*.

And so on. But a list like this does not help us much to understand how and why these artefacts came into being.

Understanding progress in design depends on our coming to understand the circumstances that help to shape new developments in design. It is not enough to know when something happened, or even who made it happen. We also need to know something about the circumstances of change. It helps us to understand progress in design if we can appreciate the kinds of circumstance that designers respond to. These include the materials and techniques available at the time, and the costs involved in terms of time and money. These in turn will be influenced by changes in society's needs.

People's attitudes will act as an influence on all these things. Attitudes will tend to determine what people want, and what they think is important. But progress in design itself changes people's attitudes, giving them new interests and desires.

Pyramid building was slow and expensive

A suspension bridge like this is only possible with high-tensile steel and other modern materials

Improving the environment

QUESTIONS

● Note some examples of progress in design since your grandparents were young. How have these changed people's attitudes?

Improving materials

The improvement of materials is an important aspect of progress in design. Iron, used for tools and weapons, had always been smelted from its ore using charcoal as a fuel. But it was discovered in the eighteenth century that coke, which can be produced from coal, made a better fuel. This allowed the building of larger furnaces called blast furnaces. The greater heat of these furnaces was enough to melt the iron completely. This new form of iron was called cast iron, because it could be poured into moulds to make castings.

Coalbrookdale in the late eighteenth century

Achievement in engineering

As the furnaces became larger, so it was possible to make larger castings. These improvements led to the world's first iron bridge, at Coalbrookdale in Shropshire. It was built in 1779 by Abraham Darby III, who was one of a family of famous ironfounders.

The bridge was cast in sections, each being floated into position and then lifted into place. With a span of over 30 m, it was a tremendous engineering achievement for the time. Users had to pay a toll, but were saved a detour of many kilometres.

The makers of the bridge still tended to rely on methods of construction borrowed from more traditional building materials such as timber. The parts were jointed together much as those of a timber bridge might have been. Clearly, the craftsmen preferred to play it safe.

The furnaces at Coalbrookdale became famous, producing much of the iron for Britain's industrial revolution.

The Ironbridge today

QUESTIONS

● Why did the Ironbridge builders prefer timber-type joints?

● What other uses do you think cast iron had?

POINT OF INTEREST

It cost more to go over the first iron bridge dead than alive – walkers went free but a hearse was charged a fee.

New techniques

Designers made use not only of new materials, but also of new techniques of construction as they made progress. The Great Exhibition of 1851 (see pages 22–3) was housed in the Crystal Palace, a remarkable building. Designed by Joseph Paxton, it was a triumph of the use of iron and glass. Using standardized and prefabricated parts – parts that were first made up and then brought to the site – it was erected in just twenty-two weeks. The great iron ribs, all made to a standard pattern, were hoisted into position using a giant, steam-powered crane. The builders worked not only by day but also at night under arc lights, which were then quite a new invention. Even the painting was done using machines.

New materials such as cast iron, and new production methods, made advances in design possible not only in bridges and buildings but in transport too. Iron was crucially important as a material for the development of the railways during the nineteenth century. It was needed for the high-pressure boilers which developed the steam power to drive the engines, and it was also needed to provide rails which were strong enough to support the weight of the engines.

Changing ways of life and work

These new developments affected people's lives. The huge expansion of the iron and coal industries, and the rapid development of new technology such as rail transport, created new kinds of work and new ways of living. Railway companies needed whole new categories of workers with new skills, particularly in engineering. The railways changed the pattern of travel and leisure too.

The Crystal Palace, 1851

The Menai Bridge, built by Thomas Telford, 1826

George Stephenson's *Locomotion*, 1825

QUESTIONS

● Why was iron such an important material in the nineteenth century?

● Why were standardized parts important for building the Crystal Palace?

POINT OF INTEREST

After the Exhibition, the Crystal Palace was taken down and rebuilt at Sydenham in southeast London, but it was destroyed by fire in 1937.

Mechanizing production

From the 1750s, mechanization began to replace more traditional methods of hand production. This was an important change, which first affected the production of textiles.

Wool and linen had been spun and woven by hand for centuries. Unlike them, cotton proved to be comparatively easy to process using mechanical methods. One of the first machines to mechanize cotton production was the cotton gin, which was invented by an ingenious American, Eli Whitney, in 1792. This stripped the cotton fibres from the seeds.

The spinning of cotton fibres into yarn had been mechanized in 1764, when James Hargreaves invented the spinning jenny. The first successful waterpowered cotton mill was built by Richard Arkwright in 1771, at Cromford in Derbyshire. Arkwright used water power to drive the mill machinery.

Using steam power

Power was essential, and although water wheels were quite effective it was the steam engine, invented by James Watt in 1776, which provided the main source of power not only for the textiles industry, but also to meet the needs of the coal and iron industries.

Again, mechanization of industries such as textiles brought important changes to the pattern of work and living. The new cotton mills provided work for many people, although conditions were often hard. Children as well as adults worked long hours in the mills.

Cheap cotton goods helped to clothe the rapidly growing population, but there were fears that the quality of design was getting poorer because of the replacement of handcraftsmanship by machines. This was a concern expressed by the Arts and Crafts designers later in the nineteenth century (see page 9).

Cotton mill in the 1840s. The hours of work were long and the unguarded machines were dangerous

Dresses made from machine-printed cotton, 1840s

QUESTIONS

● Why do you think cotton production was easier to mechanize than wool production?

● People often thought machine-printed cottons were of poorer quality than hand-printed cottons. Why do you think this was?

The growth of personal transport

These new methods not only began to change traditional patterns of work; they also made entirely new kinds of activity possible. The bicycle, which was the forerunner of the motor car as a form of mass personal transport, is an example of this.

The safety bicycle had developed into recognizably modern form by the 1880s. Again, the individual parts were produced speedily on machines specially made for each task. As with sewing machines, less skilled labour was required, which in turn lowered costs, making it possible for more people to afford the products. The cycle offered people a new freedom to enjoy leisure and cheap travel.

Safety bicycle, 1884

Model T Ford, 1912

Ford assembly line, 1914

QUESTIONS

● What advantages does mass production offer?

● Why are goods such as cycles and sewing machines so popular with people?

● Compare the Colt 45 with the eighteenth-century pistol. What main differences do you notice?

● Why do you think the later sewing machine shown here is more elaborate in design than the earlier machine?

With the development of the motor car in the late nineteenth century, these production methods had an even more profound effect. Ransome Olds, who produced the Oldsmobile shown on page 8, had achieved some success by 1905, selling over 6000 cars in that year.

But Henry Ford was to achieve even greater success than this. With his Model T, marketed in 1908, he introduced, along with the system of standardized interchangeable parts, a moving assembly line. Workers on the assembly line were responsible for the assembly of just one part of the car, which then moved on to the next worker, and so on.

This method of manufacture became known as **mass production**, and was taken up by other industries. Today many goods are manufactured using these methods.

Mass production

Mass production lowered costs, making the goods available to a larger number of people. Domestic goods such as sewing machines could help speed up everyday tasks in the home, while bicycles offered people new opportunities for leisure and travel.

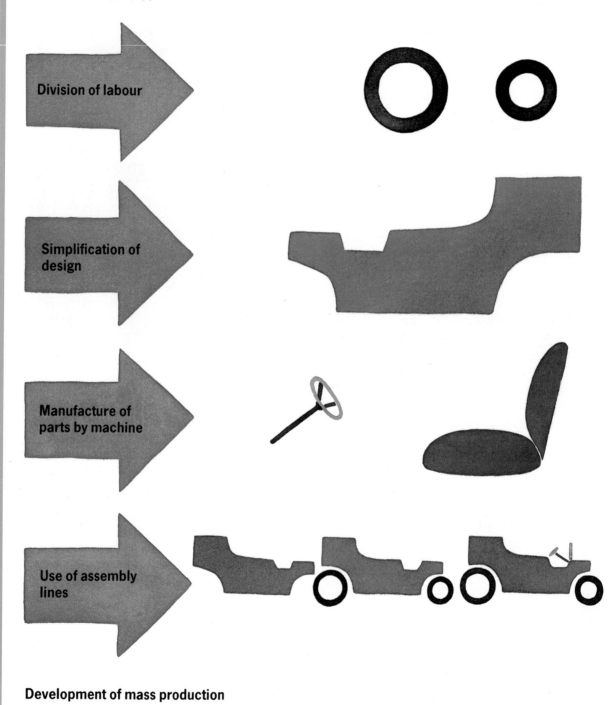

Division of labour

Simplification of design

Manufacture of parts by machine

Use of assembly lines

Development of mass production

The Great Exhibition of 1851

The nineteenth century was a time of great expansion for British designers and manufacturers. There was an air of excitement and optimism, and this was celebrated in an important event which attracted people from all over the world.

This was the Great Exhibition, held in 1851 and housed in the Crystal Palace (see page 17). One of its aims was to capture the spirit of progress in the engineering and design achievements of the day. During the five months it was open, the Exhibition attracted some 6 million visitors.

There were many artefacts on display for domestic use, such as pottery, fabrics, and furniture. The design of many of these drew on a great range of styles borrowed from different quarters – the medieval European past, as well as the far east, particularly China and Japan. Designers and manufacturers looked to a great variety of such sources, both for inspiration and also to show off their new technical skills and mechanized production methods, in products ranging from textiles machinery to machine-produced cutlery and tableware.

Other countries besides Britain exhibited wares, and some people thought that they were better designed than British products. Arts and Crafts designers (see page 9) were critical of machine-produced goods, accusing British manufacturers of poor quality in the design of their products.

Goods from the Great Exhibition, 1851

QUESTIONS

● Why did designers look to such a wide variety of styles for inspiration?

POINT OF INTEREST

Queen Victoria visited the Exhibition several times. The organizers made £186,000 profit, some of which was used to purchase land in South Kensington, London. On this land were built the Victoria and Albert Museum (1852), the Albert Hall (1867), and the Natural History Museum (1881).

ASSIGNMENTS

● Imagine there is to be another major exhibition like the Great Exhibition of 1851. What kinds of thing do you think it might contain? Make a list of your choices, saying why you think it would be important to include them.

The development of plastics

Nineteenth-century designers may have looked to a wide variety of sources for inspiration because of popular demand. Josiah Wedgwood had earlier shown how popular designs from the past could be. Also, the 1851 Exhibition was held during an age of rapid progress. It may have been the speed of change which tempted people to look back to the past, trying to recapture it.

However, many new materials and processes were developed in the later part of the nineteenth century. Among the most important of these were plastics. Materials such as horn and amber had been used for centuries. They had the property of plasticity, meaning that they could be heated and moulded or reshaped into decorative items such as combs and jewellery. These materials, though, were becoming scarce.

Items made from Bakelite

The first artificial plastics were called semi-synthetics, because they were synthesized from natural substances such as acids and woodflour. Two of the most important of these semi-synthetics were **Parkesine** and **celluloid**. Parkesine (called after its inventor, Alexander Parkes) was popular as a substitute for ivory and horn. Celluloid, which was an improvement on the rather brittle Parkesine, was a very good substitute for tortoiseshell. These new materials made possible a great variety of products at affordable prices – combs, boxes, and jewellery, as well as pens, knife handles, cheap cutlery, and toys.

New forms of plastic

In the 1920s, chemists discovered that an entirely new range of plastics could be made from the chemicals in coal, oil, and natural gas. These new plastics were called synthetics.

This discovery was largely the work of a German chemist called Hermann Staudinger, who put forward the idea that plastics were composed of giant molecules in chains of as much as 1000 atoms in length. So he began research on coal, oil, and natural gas, which have chemicals made up of long chains of atoms. Staudinger showed his ideas were sound when he succeeded in synthesizing rubber, which had previously been obtained from certain plants. From his work came modern synthetic plastics such as **nylon** and **polythene**.

Plastics ware from the 1950s and 1960s

QUESTIONS

● What opportunities do you think the new plastic materials gave designers?

● Look at the items in the photographs on these pages. Which of them would have been difficult to make in materials other than plastic? Give reasons for this.

Technologists drew upon the ideas of scientists such as Staudinger to develop new plastics, in large enough amounts to make the mass production of new kinds of plastics ware possible. Since the arrival of plastics, designers have had available to them materials which are durable, can be easily formed, coloured, and decorated, and which in many cases have proven superior to the traditional materials they have replaced.

Plastics have made possible a whole way of life which would be unthinkable without them. They continue to open up new possibilities for designers everywhere.

Contemporary plastics ware

Progress in design

New developments in design are often linked to advances in the use of materials and techniques, and these advances are frequently linked in turn to changing needs and attitudes. These, together with the growth in population, have opened up new markets for a great variety of consumer goods.

The shaping of the new production processes in the last century was due not just to new ideas in science and technology, but also to people's desires and aspirations. The great wave of new products coming from the assembly lines gave people opportunities for entirely new ways of living. Design in the twentieth century has focused as much on people's desires and fantasies as on their needs.

QUESTIONS

● Give some examples of how people's changing needs and attitudes might affect manufacturers and designers.

● Give as many examples as you can of new products that have given people opportunities for new ways of living. How have they done this?

Growth of plastics production, 1860–1985

Source: *Social Trends HMSO 1990*

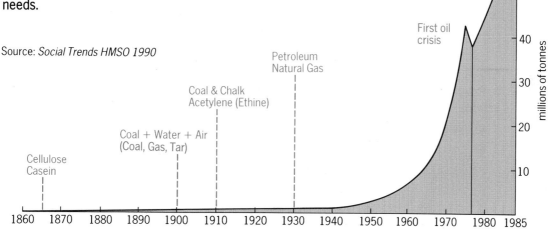
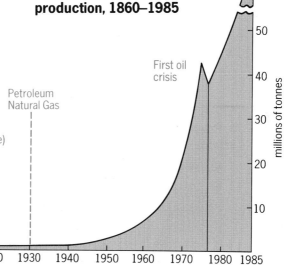

Designing with new materials

Living with change

As the twentieth century has advanced, so progress in design has become increasingly dominated by the growth of **consumerism**. We now live in a consumer society, which in a way needs to consume in order to survive. The sheer size of the market for all kinds of goods, from cars, TVs, and fridge-freezers to clothes, jewellery, and cosmetics, has itself created problems for designers.

One reason for this is that people have not only needs, but also desires and fantasies. Designers have come increasingly to recognize that these too need to be catered for. A car may symbolize power and success. A house may symbolize wealth and social status. Clothes may signal taste, sense of style, and individuality.

Ford Edsell, 1958

Sinclair Trike, 1986

In judging public tastes in such matters, designers and manufacturers may sometimes make costly mistakes. One of the reasons for the failure of the car (shown above) was that public taste began to swing away from the extravagantly styled cars that had been popular in the early 1950s.

Products like cars cost huge sums to develop, and it is vital for manufacturers and designers to judge the potential market correctly. Some products, like the Rubik cube, have a spectacular but brief success, while others, such as the Workmate, sell well for many years.

Rubik cube

Workmate, 1979

QUESTIONS

● Think of reasons why products like the Rubik cube have a brief success, while others such as the Workmate remain successful for a long period.

● Give possible reasons why the Sinclair Trike (shown above) was unsuccessful.

ASSIGNMENTS

● Progress in design and technology can bring change for everyone. Computers are a familiar example.

a) Make a list of the kinds of job you think this new technology has created.

b) List the kinds of skill that workers in these jobs might need.

c) Describe the changes to everyday life in the home that computers have introduced.

d) Suggest ways in which computers can help in important areas of industry such as design and manufacture.

Specialist designers

In the past, designers often worked on single, one-off projects for the wealthy. Today, however, designers usually work on designs which can be manufactured for many customers. The products they design are mass produced and marketed on a large scale. This is called mass marketing.

Designers may work individually, or in a team. They may work as consultants for a number of clients who hire them to produce particular designs, or they may be employed by one company, working on the whole range of that company's products.

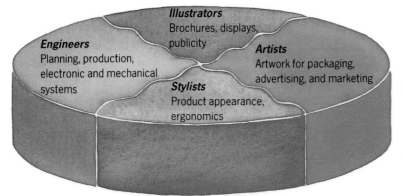

Illustrators
Brochures, displays, publicity

Engineers
Planning, production, electronic and mechanical systems

Artists
Artwork for packaging, advertising, and marketing

Stylists
Product appearance, ergonomics

Design today is usually teamwork involving different specialists

Because most manufacturers produce goods for large markets, several different design specialisms may be involved. Some designers may work on the product, while others may be responsible for designing the manufacturing systems which produce it. Many expensive tools and machines are needed to produce a motor car, for example. A manufacturing system for a product like this will require different specialist designers to develop it, such as electronics and robotics engineers.

Many products will also require **packaging**, and designers work on the design both of the package and also of the system to manufacture the package. The food industry provides many examples of this kind of design activity.

Marketing also requires the expertise of designers to work on displays, advertising, and the design and layout of the stores in which the goods are sold.

Goods like these are produced by expensive manufacturing tools

Packaging machinery in operation

QUESTIONS
● Why do designers today need to specialize in different kinds of work?

Customers' needs

In the intense competition of today's markets, designers have to try to ensure that they are meeting the customers' needs before putting designs into production. With the high costs involved, mistakes can be expensive.

One way of finding out what customers need is to ask them. This may seem obvious, but people often may not know what they really need.

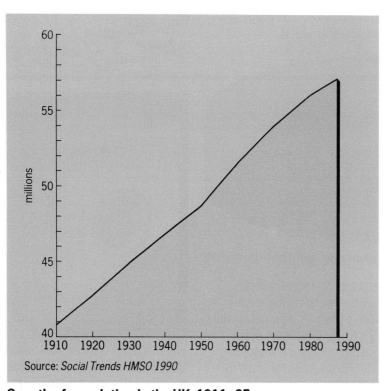

Source: *Social Trends HMSO 1990*

Growth of population in the UK, 1911–85

Market researchers are often employed by manufacturers to find out people's probable needs. They interview a sample of people, and then base estimates of demand for different products on the replies they get.

Another approach is to study official records like the **National Census** statistics. From such records, it is possible to assess changing trends in the pattern of everyday living, as well as the changing make-up of the population. From this kind of information, people's likely future needs can be estimated.

ASSIGNMENTS

● As a student of design and technology, you have been commissioned by your school magazine to write a short article on design for today's teenagers. Write a draft of this article, outlining the ways in which you think design concerns young people, and what they consider is most important about design for them.

● Market research is an important way of finding out what kinds of product people buy, and what their needs are. Design surveys aimed at finding out:

a) what kind of school canteen service pupils in your school would like.

b) what kind of school library service pupils in your school would like.

Try in each case to frame questions which will give as much useful information as possible about ways of providing a good service.

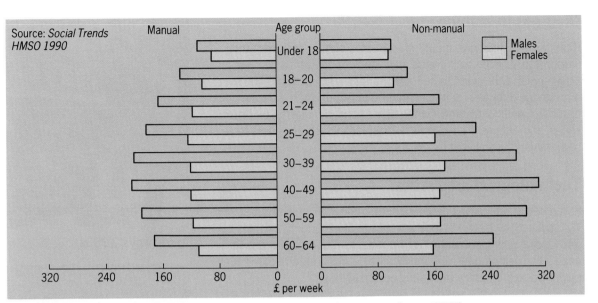

Source: *Social Trends HMSO 1990*

Average gross weekly earnings of full-time employees by age and sex, 1987

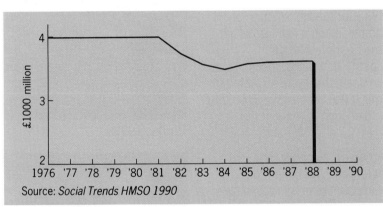

Source: *Social Trends HMSO 1990*

Expenditure on books and newspapers in the UK, 1976–88

The demand for some kinds of product, such as furniture, may change only slightly, while the demand for other products, such as video recorders or fashion clothing, may tend to rise and fall. The demand for some items may depend on how well off people are, or on interest rates for borrowing money.

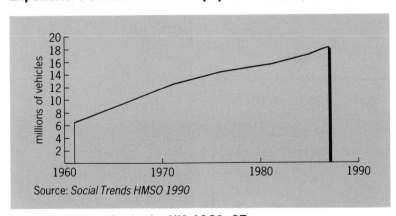

Source: *Social Trends HMSO 1990*

Growth of car sales in the UK, 1961–87

QUESTIONS

● Why does the demand for some goods tend to rise and fall?

● The UK population is levelling off, but spending on goods still goes up. Why is this?

● Which population groups offer the best markets for goods?

Developing the product

Changes in fashion

Changes in fashion give plenty of examples of how designers may respond to, or even help create, new kinds of customer demand. Designers may respond to cultural changes – for example, the emergence of reggae or heavy metal – by supplying the demand for particular kinds of fashion. On the other hand, mini-skirts, platform shoes, and denims are examples of fashions which designers have been mainly responsible for creating.

Technological innovation

Some new products will depend on technological innovation. Josiah Wedgwood (see page 19) took advantage of expanding markets by introducing new manufacturing methods, as did Henry Ford (see page 21). Their pioneering approach helped to create demand for new products, and new marketing opportunities.

New inventions

Sometimes, new inventions pave the way for the introduction of entirely new kinds of product. For example, electric lighting, which we today take for granted, only became possible with the development of the first successful electric light bulbs. Joseph Swan and Thomas Edison both succeeded in doing this by 1881. Although the idea had been known for some time, it was technically difficult to produce a vacuum inside the bulb good enough to prevent the filament burning away.

New inventions can also provide designers with opportunities for a complete rethinking of existing products. The invention of the transistor in the 1950s led to the replacement of bulky radio valves with much smaller components, resulting in small portable radios which found a ready market.

Teddy boys, 1950s

Punks, 1970s

Edison light bulb, 1890s

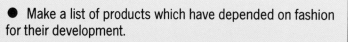

QUESTIONS

● Make a list of products which have depended on fashion for their development.

● Why are innovation and invention important for new design?

● Research the 'history' of the vacuum light blub.

Successful product marketing depends on a great degree of standardization. This helps to make savings on materials costs and production time, and also helps to make the product more saleable. This was an idea which was developed during the eighteenth century (see page 20).

During the nineteenth century, many components were standardized. Among these were the screw threads for nuts and bolts, which most things from washing machines to aeroplanes rely on.

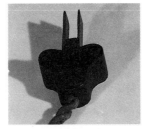 

An early plug for electrical appliances, and today's square-pin plug

Electrical goods

During the early twentieth century, when electricity began to become a major source of energy in the home, lack of standardization led to a bewildering array of components, none of which would fit one another. This discouraged people from buying electrical goods. Manufacturers again had to get together to agree on standards for wiring systems, plugs, and sockets. Design and manufacturing standards were also set to make the equipment safer.

Products such as TV sets are mostly made from standardized components

Office equipment such as this typewriter uses standardized sizes of paper

Recording equipment

More recently, problems have occurred over the design of high fidelity recording equipment, with compact disc players challenging older forms of disc recording. Even the compact disc system of recording could be replaced by digital audio tape systems, which could offer the same quality as a compact disc, but on a cheaper tape system.

The customer may benefit from this kind of competition, but for industry to produce a range of viable products, engineering systems such as this need to be standardized.

POINT OF INTEREST

The British Standards Institute is an independent organization which sets standards of quality and safety for most everyday products. There are thousands of these standards, and they apply not only to products but also to the materials from which they are made.

QUESTIONS

● Why would the lack of standardization have held back the development of new products?

● Does standardization have any disadvantages?

Standardization again

Product manufacture

The marketing of many everyday products is only possible with systems which control and carry out the stages in the manufacture, and even the packaging of the product.

Production in large quantities

As an example, the marketing of canned drinks involves the production of millions of cans per week in this country. The cans are produced in stages, using computer controlled machinery which:

- forms the can from a flat sheet of metal;
- prints the label on the can;
- fills the can with drink;
- seals the lid on the can;
- provides quality control.

This type of automatic, assembly line production system is a development from the earlier work of the pioneering car manufacturer Henry Ford (see page 21).

Flexible manufacturing systems

Computers are also increasingly being used to control machines for small quantity production. For example, the manufacture of fitted kitchens can now be tailored to suit the needs of individual customers. Each customer can choose from a range of standard parts which can be put together in any combination desired.

This manufacturing system is flexible, because it can produce the exact number of parts required to make up any individual order. There is no waste, and the manufacturer does not need to keep large numbers of parts in stock, so the system is also very economic.

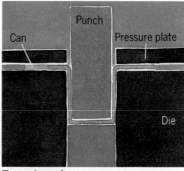
Forming the cans

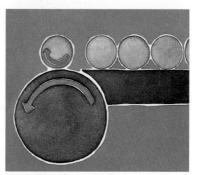
Printing the labels

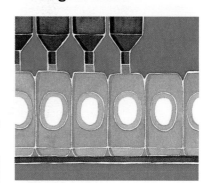
Filling the cans

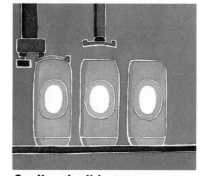
Sealing the lids on

ASSIGNMENTS

● Imagine you are a successful product designer working in your chosen field for a large manufacturer. You have been asked by the company to report on what the next big seller in your field is likely to be. Prepare a report for your marketing director, to include:

a) an outline design for the product.

b) a brief description of the stages in its production.

c) if the product is to be packaged, a suitable package design for it.

d) an outline for a suitable advertising campaign to sell your product.

Costs are an important consideration in the design and development of any product. An automated assembly line, for example, is very expensive to build. So the size of the potential market will have an important bearing on its installation.

Materials

Material costs are important too. In the production of a drinks can, even a small amount of wasted material per can would have an effect on overall production costs. Designers have to be careful to minimize this kind of waste.

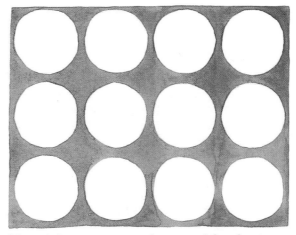

Materials cost money: the rest of the sheet from which the drinks cans are stamped is waste

New technology

Invention and innovation also affect the economics of production. For example, the design of today's home computer depends on the latest technology. The heart of the computer is the silicon chip, a minute sandwich of silicon and germanium which has a vast number of circuits etched into it by ultraviolet light. The chip replaces older circuit designs which were much larger and more cumbersome, and required expensive materials and skilled labour for their manufacture.

TV components, 1950s   **TV components, 1990s**

The cost of change

Reduction in materials costs, labour, and production time have brought computer production costs down, and made it possible for many people to buy home computers, as well as a wide range of other goods produced by the microelectronics industry. A high volume of sales gives the manufacturer a return on the often very high development costs.

But new technology like this can threaten people's jobs, or require them to retrain for new kinds of work. Redundancy and retraining are 'hidden' costs, but they still affect the prices we pay for the things we want. New technology requires investment not only in expensive machines, but also in the training people need to equip them with vital new skills.

Computer, 1960s. The personal computer alongside has a similar output

QUESTIONS

● What advantages have products such as home computers brought to people?

● Redundancy and retraining are 'hidden' costs. What other 'hidden' costs might the introduction of new technology involve?

Packaging

The drinks can is usually thrown away when finished with, even though it is the product of some advanced engineering design. Like most of today's packaging, it is regarded as disposable.

Packaging is important for two main reasons. It allows the product to be transported from manufacturer to customer, and it also serves to display or advertise the product. Designers pay careful attention to both of these aspects. The package may sometimes be more expensive than the product, and can be an important selling point.

Product image

The importance of effective packaging was recognized early in the twentieth century, when companies such as Coca-Cola realized that a distinctive style might help their sales. In 1916, Coca-Cola came up with the design of bottle still used today, which did much to establish the company's image with the public. Many other drinks producers have since followed suit. Other domestic products such as soap, polish, and matches also began to receive the packaging treatment from around the turn of the century, again helping to establish a product image important for sales.

Modern plastics have revolutionized packaging for many of today's products. Many foods are marketed using plastic containers, as also are polishes, cleaners, and personal care products. Plastics are ideally suited for making airtight, leakproof containers, and can be moulded in eye-catching forms and colours. Other plastics can be used as protective packaging for the transport of fragile goods such as electronics equipment.

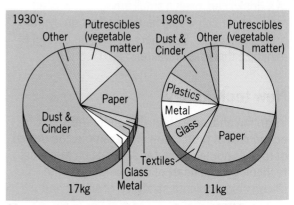

Changes in composition and size of UK household waste

Threats to the environment

However, packaging can create problems – for example, litter, or the disposal of discarded containers. These can create environmental hazards. Designers, manufacturers, and the public may need to take such problems more seriously in the future.

QUESTIONS

● How does packaging help to establish a product's image?

● Suggest ways in which the problems that packaging causes, such as litter, might be solved.

The package can be an effective form of advertising. Manufacturers need to get their products noticed, of course, and advertising is the main way of achieving this.

Early catalogues and posters set out both to convey information and also to try to create the right kind of image. The challenge of getting the message across to the public became more urgent as competition increased. In the 1920s, the gas and electricity industries were in keen competition with one another. Much product advertising was aimed at the housewife, and electrical goods manufacturers projected an image of cleanliness and futuristic efficiency. Gas responded by stressing cheapness and reliability.

Electrical Development Association poster, 1920s

Persuading us to buy

Designers often aim to persuade us through that kind of advertising. To have their product, the advertisements imply, is to be happy, contented, or successful – just as the people in the advertisement appear to be. Television and radio are very powerful means of product advertising, and designers of TV advertising spend a great deal of time and money creating the images that they hope will persuade the public to buy.

But, of course, advertising may also be intended to carry useful information about the product. We have to learn to discriminate, and not be taken in too easily.

Protecting the public

Advertisers have to abide by a code which requires advertisements to be legal, decent, honest, and truthful. People can complain to the Advertising Standards Authority if they see advertising material they believe breaks this code.

QUESTIONS

● List the ways in which each of the advertisements shown here tries to sell its product.

● Why is TV such a powerful advertising medium?

● Some forms of advertising are banned. List as many as you can, and say why you think they are banned.

Retailing

In pre-industrial times, producers took their goods to the local open-air market. Customers would flock into the town on market days to buy the things they needed. Today, although open-air markets survive as a colourful feature of town life, there are other means of getting the goods to the customers. Since the last century, the high street shop has gradually replaced the older style marketplace. In more recent years, supermarkets and chainstores have begun to take over.

Store design

The layout and appearance of shops and stores has increasingly become the concern of designers, who are hired to help create a distinctive style. The company sign or logo is a guide to quick recognition outside the store, while inside much effort may be put in to create the right atmosphere. Lighting, layout, and ease of access are all important.

Creating a setting

Household items such as furniture or crockery tend to look better when set in surroundings made to look like a home. Other kinds of retail outlet, such as garden centres, also try to create 'natural' settings for plants and garden furniture in order to attract attention and persuade people to buy.

Large stores need to arrange similar types of goods together, too, so that customers can find them easily or see them demonstrated.

QUESTIONS

● Retail outlets usually display goods and products in the kinds of setting they are designed to be used in. Why does this help to sell them?

● Suggest ways in which designers try to sell products such as clothes or jewellery.

Services such as transport, banks, and building societies may also need the skills of designers to help them get ideas across to the public. A transport system such as the London Underground carries around one million passengers daily, and provides a vital service for travellers. Passengers need information about how to reach their destination, and designers may play an important part here.

Mapping London Underground

When the London Underground map was redesigned in the 1930s, it simplified the older design, and was much easier to follow. Today's map is closely based on the 1930s one, and the idea has since been copied around the world. Station signs were improved by designers in the 1930s too, making it much easier to identify stations in busy streets, or from moving trains. Station layout and passenger information signs have also been given attention by designers, to make travelling easier.

London welcomes several million tourists each year, apart from the daily rush of workers and shoppers, so this kind of design activity is very important. Effective design can help to carry information quickly and clearly to the public.

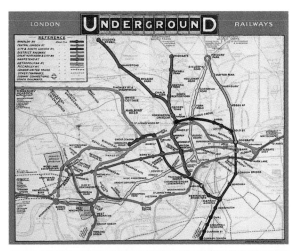

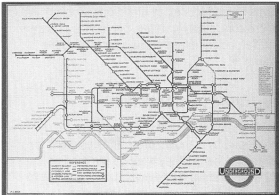

The old London Underground map and the redesigned map, 1930s

Creating an identity

The public needs other kinds of service too, and again, designers can help. Banks and building societies, for example, need to create a clear image in the mind of the public in order to advertise their services. Signs and logos, together with the treatment of interior decoration and furnishings, can all help to create a distinctive kind of style which the public can readily identify, and recognize as a particular type of service.

QUESTIONS

● Why is the redesigned map of the London Underground better than the old one (both shown here)?

● In what ways does the design and layout of the bank in the photographs help customers?

Looking to the future

In helping manufacturers to market their products, designers have a demanding task. It includes the design, development, production, advertising, distribution, and selling of a wide range of goods and services. All of these things need to be carefully attended to if designs are to succeed, and customers are to get what they need.

But in addition, manufacturers and designers (who in some cases are one and the same) have to try to see into the future. They need to try to foresee future needs, and predict likely trends. In thinking about this, it is worth considering some of the products we now take for granted, but which weren't around even twenty years ago – which in terms of product design is not long! Pocket calculators, digital watches, personal computers, and flatpack furniture are just some possible examples.

The need to plan ahead

These products were being planned and developed by manufacturers and designers for some time before they were on the market. Manufacturers and designers have therefore to think well ahead, since it may take years to develop a new product. The best and the most adventurous design will depend on designers and manufacturers being ready and willing to take on this kind of challenge.

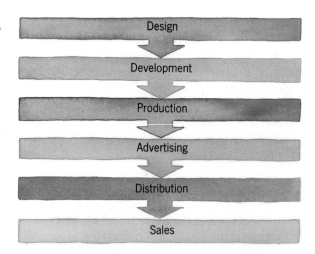

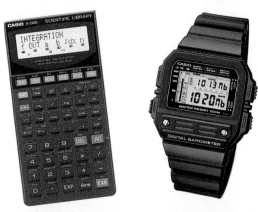

The customer can take flatpack furniture away and assemble it at home. This saves on labour costs

QUESTIONS

● Make a note of all the products you can think of that were not around twenty years ago. Research this by asking older friends and family members, and visiting a museum with a modern collection if possible.

● What do you think are the most important advances in design during the last twenty years?

In the environment

Design has come to play an increasingly important part in our environment. One reason for this is that technological progress has greatly extended our power over the environment. Another reason is that our towns and cities have become more complicated places to live in than they were in the past.

The environment includes houses, roads, factories, shopping centres, parks, power stations, and the surrounding countryside. Design decisions about the environment involve many people, including architects, planners, and civil engineers, as well as local councils and central government.

The design and construction of buildings, power stations, or transport systems needs experts such as **civil engineers** or **architects**. But decisions about what to do are often controversial, and can lead to public enquiries, at which people who are not experts but who are concerned about the proposals may give their views. It can sometimes take several years to reach a decision which is acceptable to everyone.

People have become more aware of the dangers to the environment from pollution, and the destruction of natural resources such as the rain forests. Environmental scientists specialize in studying the climate, oceans, and atmosphere. They can advise on the likely effects that different forms of pollution may have on the environment, and also how best to look after the world's resources.

QUESTIONS

● List some of the benefits and some of the disadvantages that technology has created for the environment.

● Why is it important to look after the world's natural resources?

Central government
Pass laws, set standards, hold enquiries, set up royal commissions

Local government
Enforce regulations, make by-laws, oversee planning

Industry and commerce
Respond to society's needs, try to influence public and government

Health and safety inspectorate
See that laws and regulations are complied with

Local authorities
Employ public health inspectors and medical officers to check standards

Pressure groups
Put pressure on government, industry, and public to bring about improvements

Some of the people and organizations concerned with the environment

Urbanization in the nineteenth century

The concern over public health

In 1842, Edwin Chadwick, who was a leading campaigner for improvements in public health, recommended improvements to the design of sewers. He also pressed for more effective treatment of sewage to avoid contamination of fresh water. Chadwick and his colleagues showed, by careful detective work, that outbreaks of cholera could be traced back to contaminated water.

Writers such as Charles Dickens also stirred the consciences of the better off with vivid accounts of the hardships suffered by the poor. Much of the housing at the time was of poor quality, built back-to-back with no proper ventilation. There was no proper refuse disposal. Streets and courtyards were often filthy.

Legislation for reform

A major difficulty in the way of reform was the lack of any organized planning laws. There was also resistance from landlords and factory owners. But the work of people such as Chadwick led eventually to new legislation. This involved, among other things, the appointment of public health inspectors. These inspectors had the power to force people to reduce pollution and improve property.

The River Thames was very unhealthy in the early nineteenth century

	1849	1853–4	1866
All London Average	62	46	18
Bermondsey	161	179	6
St. George Southwark	164	121	1
Newington	144	112	3
Rotherhithe	205	165	9
Kensington	24	38	4
St. George – Hanover Square	18	33	2
St. Martin-in-the-Fields	37	20	5
St. James – Westminster	16	142	5

Deaths from cholera per 10,000 of population in the London area 1849–66

QUESTIONS

● Why were improvements to the design of sewage systems and water supplies so important?

● Why was change resisted by some people?

Installing new sewers, 1860s

A large number of terraced and semi-detached houses were built in the early part of the twentieth century. Most of these houses were improvements on nineteenth-century housing. They were well designed and soundly built, and often had a bathroom, unlike much of the earlier housing.

However, after World War I, population growth again began to put pressures on cities and towns. This led to the beginnings of urban sprawl, with large areas of **ribbon development** springing up along roads leading into towns. Much of this housing was of a poor standard, and critics described it as 'jerry building'. This was a term which first came into use during the nineteenth century, and meant hastily erected, poorly designed houses built from inferior materials.

Modernist architecture

Some of these later designs were built in what became known as the modernist style. This was being pioneered by leading European architects such as Le Corbusier (French) and Mies van der Rohe (German). Modernist architecture aimed at creating not merely a style of building, but also a whole new way of urban living. Le Corbusier declared that the house was 'a machine for living in'. It was to be designed and built to be as efficient and economic as possible and promote modern, convenient living.

Ribbon development, 1930s

Isokon flats, Hampstead, north London: designed by Wells Coates, 1933

> **QUESTIONS**
>
> ● What advantages/disadvantages do flats have over houses?
>
> ● Do modern housing estates 'work'?

Early twentieth-century terraced housing

De Dageraad flats, Amsterdam, 1918

High Point flats, London, 1938

The garden cities

A few pioneers in the late nineteenth century decided to create improved conditions by building entirely new towns out in the countryside. One of these early pioneers, Ebenezer Howard, believed that garden cities should be built on land held in trust for the community. These cities were to be surrounded by a green belt – an area of land kept free of building in order to provide some open space.

Port Sunlight, Cheshire

Ebenezer Howard helped form the Garden City Association, which led to the development of Letchworth and Welwyn Garden City, both in Hertfordshire, just north of London. The garden city ideal was also pursued by industrialists such as Lord Leverhulme, the Rowntree family, and the Cadbury family. Each of these built housing estates for their employees, intended to serve as good examples of town planning and architectural design.

Letchworth, Hertfordshire

Bournville, Birmingham

Community by design

Through a careful mix of houses, and amenities such as schools, shops, hospitals, libraries, and churches, together with good roads and open spaces, garden cities sought to set new standards of planning and design. Buildings were of simple but sound construction, and leading architects contributed to their designs.

Hampstead Garden Suburb, in north London, was another example of the new style of town planning in the early twentieth century. London County Council also set about developing various designs of cottage estates, such as Becontree in east London. At their best, these new developments were created with careful attention to choice of building materials, with roads designed for safe use, giving good access. But estates such as Becontree, although providing homes for many families, did little to improve the urban environment.

Hampstead Garden Suburb, north London

Becontree Estate, east London

Q U E S T I O N S

● Why do you think rich industrialists like the Cadbury family wanted to build houses for their workers?

● What differences do you notice between the Becontree Estate and Hampstead Garden Suburb (both shown here)?

A S S I G N M E N T S

● Imagine that you are on the committee of designers and planners who are drawing up proposals for an out-of-town shopping centre in your area. Draw up a list of the design and planning problems the committee might have to solve, and suggest solutions. Make careful sketch plans of the shopping centre, clearly showing features such as the layout of the store, access for customer's vehicles, car parking for customers, access for delivery of goods, provision for the disabled, and other customer services, such as a refreshment area, a play area for young children, petrol and diesel sales, etc.

The new towns

After World War II, the urgent need to rehouse people in bomb-damaged cities led to a great increase in the building of flats and apartments. These were constructed using steel framing and reinforced concrete. They became known as **high-rise** or tower blocks, because they could be built much taller than was possible with more traditional building methods. Since they could house more people in a given area, they were also a more efficient use of land than low-rise building.

Yet despite this mass housing, the post-war population boom forced the government to look to the creation of **new towns**, rather like the earlier garden cities. New towns such as Hemel Hempstead, Basingstoke, and Basildon took overspill population from London. They sought to create a balance of housing, amenities, and industry by means of careful planning from the initial building stage right through to the completed town. A particularly well-known example of this is Milton Keynes.

New opportunities for all

People were attracted to the new towns not only by the opportunity of better housing, but also by the prospect of jobs on the new, purpose-built industrial estates. Shopping and leisure amenities also offered quick and easy access. Schools, colleges, and dental and doctors' surgeries could all be incorporated into the town plans at the design stage. This gave the specialist designers responsible (architects and town **planners**) good opportunities to create better living conditions for all the people.

Thamesmead Estate, London, 1968

Milton Keynes shopping centre

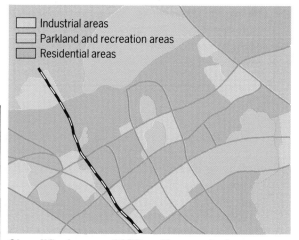

☐ Industrial areas
☐ Parkland and recreation areas
☐ Residential areas

Simplified map of Milton Keynes today

QUESTIONS

● Make a list of the advantages and disadvantages that high-rise dwellings offer people.

● What interesting features do you notice about Milton Keynes from the map shown here?

Creating better living conditions can be a difficult challenge to meet. For example, tower blocks are designed to house people efficiently, but they pose some typical problems:

■ vandalized lights and lifts;

■ lack of privacy for residents;

■ lack of adequate play space;

■ inadequate provision for the elderly and infirm.

The need to design housing which caters for the demands of everyday living is an important objective.

People have become more aware of the need to try to improve the quality of the whole environment, but this can be difficult to achieve. It means paying careful attention to the needs not only of different groups such as children, the elderly, pedestrians, and motorists, but also of people needing access to shops, stores, banks, medical centres, and so on.

Creating harmony

Architects and town planners strive to create a careful balance between these different – and often conflicting – needs. They try to create a harmony between older buildings and new ones, focusing on appearance as well as convenience, safety, freedom from noise, pollution, and so on. Careful use of building materials, plenty of trees, flowers, and shrubs, seating, and lighting all help to improve the urban environment.

QUESTIONS

● Make a note of the ways in which the designer of the pedestrianized area in the photograph has tried to make it pleasant and easy to use.

● What have the architects done to blend old buildings with newer ones in the city centre right?

Balancing needs

Some mass housing projects have failed to meet people's needs

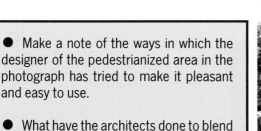

Pedestrianized area, Norwich

New development blended with older buildings

The street scene

For people on the move, road and traffic signs are an important and useful feature of the environment. General information signs are also useful for pedestrians. Shop signs and advertisements can be informative and helpful, if they are designed to fit into the surroundings. Care needs to be taken with their design and siting.

Common faults which may be found in any town can be seen in the photograph here. The traffic and information signs are cluttered and confusing, and route direction signs are placed in unsightly positions which also make them difficult to read.

Retaining local character

Shops need to advertise their presence, and advertisers need to get people's attention. But this can be done without creating an unsightly mess. A national chainstore can still retain its identity without ruining the character of the local architecture.

Retaining local character?

Advertisers can also get their message across without dwarfing the rest of the environment. As long as some attention is given to the way in which advertisements relate to their surroundings, there need be no clash.

Creating atmosphere

Lighting is another important part of the environment. Both pedestrians and motorists need to get around safely during the hours of darkness. But lighting also has great potential for creating mood, and bringing the city to life at night.

Advertising: Piccadilly, London

Many other things play some part in helping to create the right kind of environment. Well-designed telephone kiosks, bus shelters, and litter bins can be just as important as large-scale features, such as buildings.

British Telecom telephone kiosks

Big Ben at night

QUESTIONS

● Make a note of the bad features you can see in the traffic and information signs above.

● Compare the advertising displays above. Decide which is better, giving the reasons for your decision.

Industry supplies goods for our domestic market, and for markets abroad. But not all industrial activity is concerned with making goods for sale. Service industries, such as gas, electricity, and coal, provide us with basic energy needs. These needs are not only for the home, but also for industrial production and transport.

There is a lot of industrial activity in and around towns and cities. Factories need to be conveniently sited so that people can get to work, and both factories and power stations need to be close to roads and railways in order to receive supplies of materials and to dispatch goods.

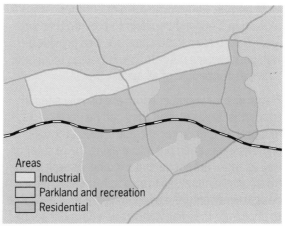

Areas
☐ Industrial
☐ Parkland and recreation
☐ Residential

Simplified map of Basildon today

Controlling industrial pollution

Much government legislation has been aimed at removing the effects of industrial pollution. The Clean Air Act of 1956 dramatically reduced air pollution, which until then had been a common cause of death, particularly among old people during the winter smogs which used to descend on cities. More recently, the Control of Pollution Act of 1974 has provided for more efficient refuse collection and disposal, and also for the control of water pollution in rivers and tidal waters around the British coast.

Factories today are generally sited in industrial areas away from houses, and are subject to controls aimed at preventing pollution by industrial wastes. Domestic waste is often buried in landfill sites, which when filled can be landscaped or built on. Some local authorities are looking at ways of reclaiming domestic waste, such as glass, metals, and paper.

QUESTIONS

● What do you notice about the development of Basildon from the map above?

● Much domestic waste (newspaper, glass, tins, etc.) could be reclaimed. What problems need to be solved in achieving this?

Factory estate, Isle of Dogs, London

Chemical works

Landfill estate

Industry

Parks and amenities

Most people enjoy some form of outdoor relaxation. Parkland can help to provide this, and most British towns and cities are well provided with parks, which cater for a wide range of leisure activities for people of all ages.

Play areas for young children are usually sited in residential areas so that they can be easily reached on foot. In recent years, much thought and effort has been put into making these safer as well as more attractive and exciting. As well as the traditional sandpits, swings, and roundabouts, well-designed adventure playgrounds are now available to challenge the imagination and energy of young children.

As well as the ever popular sporting activities such as swimming and ball games, some local authorities now provide additional amenities such as ice rinks, roller dromes, and skateboard parks.

Recreation for the whole family

Some people prefer their outdoor activities to be more leisurely, and many towns provide golf courses. Open parkland on the outskirts of towns can provide a pleasant means of relaxation for the whole family. We also have **national parks**, such as Snowdonia or the Yorkshire Dales. These are large areas of countryside in which all activities such as farming, building, or industry are kept under careful control, so as to preserve the areas' natural beauty for the enjoyment of everyone. In national parkland, design activity mainly takes the form of planning for open-air recreations (such as boating and climbing) and the study of plants and wildlife.

ASSIGNMENTS

● Your local council has approached the young people in your area with proposals to build a new open-air leisure park specially catering for young people's needs.

a) Draw up a list of the features you think the park should contain.

b) Make a plan of the park showing all these features, paying careful attention to safety aspects.

c) Draw up a detailed design for *one* of these features.

Travel by road

John McAdam (1756–1836), inventor of modern road surfacing

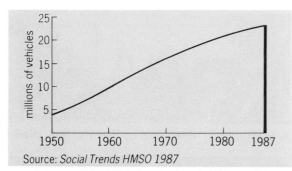

Growth in motorized road traffic, 1951–87

Source: *Social Trends HMSO 1987*

Building a motorway

Spaghetti Junction, Birmingham

Roads are a vital part of our environment. Today, there are some 260,000 km of classified roads forming a network that gives access to virtually every part of the country. The motor car, together with other vehicles, has been responsible for the tremendous growth in our road system which has taken place since the early twentieth century.

Much effort has gone into developing the civil engineering technology required for bridges, tunnels, and road surfacing, as well as traffic control systems. Using reinforced concrete, engineers can create bridges, flyovers, and complicated motorway intersections. Road building has come a long way since John McAdam, the nineteenth-century road builder.

Benefits and disadvantages

Roads give people the freedom to travel anywhere, door to door. They also permit the transport of goods right to the place where they are needed.

However, roads built to solve one set of traffic problems may create others. Vehicles can be noisy and cause pollution. Roads take up land which may be needed for other uses, such as housing, particularly in busy urban areas. New roads also tend to create even heavier demands, which often far outstrip the original calculations of the planners.

Planners have the difficult task of estimating likely future demand for roads. Engineers have the equally difficult task of trying to design and build roads to withstand today's traffic.

QUESTIONS

● List as many reasons as you can think of which may have contributed to the increase in road traffic this century.

● What advantages might roads have over rail for transporting goods? Does rail transport offer any advantages over roads?

49

Cities and the future

A vision of the future designed by Sant' Elia, 1916

The quality of the environment is important to all of us, wherever we live, work, or play. Architects, planners, artists, and even film directors have all had visions of what the environment could be like in the future. Some of these ideas may seem strange to us now. But everyone actually involved in environmental design has to try to foresee the future. This is because of the need to plan ahead for population growth, changing needs, and so on. In a way, the future is already with us. Because it takes years of planning and effort to bring changes, much of what the future environment will look like is already on the drawing boards of architects, engineers, and planners.

A 'walking city' designed by Ron Herron, 1964

Designing control systems

Designers play an important part not only in the design of the environment, but also in its control. System designers are experts who may combine computing skills with skills in other areas, such as town planning, railway engineering, water, or electricity supply. They work, for example, on the design of systems such as that used by British Rail to control the signalling equipment, or on systems for controlling traffic flow in busy towns and cities. Without sophisticated control systems such as these, traffic on rail and road would grind to a halt.

British Rail signals control room

Controlling motorway traffic by computer

Facing the future

As cities and towns become ever more complex, so the design specialists whose skills help shape the environment play an increasingly important part. Design in the environment is very much a matter of teamwork involving several different areas of skills. But there is a growing need for environmental designers with a broad range of skills to help cope with the demands of the future.

Variety in design?

Production cars like this are available in a range of specifications

Even the wealthy like to customize their cars

'Mix and match' furniture

Standardized designs

The huge costs involved in the design, development, and marketing of complex products, such as cars or domestic appliances, can create quite a challenge when trying to satisfy individual customers. Henry Ford, the pioneer of mass produced cars (see page 21), realized that standardizing the product could bring costs down. Yet Ford found in the 1920s that his sales were declining. The public were getting tired of the same old designs.

Competitors like General Motors had shown that the public liked a choice of different designs of car, and were also quite willing to trade in their old models for new ones with improved performance or stylistic changes. Although this went against Ford's original aim of trying to keep costs as low as possible, he was forced to follow suit in order to compete.

Creating variety

This kind of problem can present designers and manufacturers with a dilemma. Mass production brings down costs, but customers demand variety. One way of getting round this is to offer customers a 'basic' product which can then be supplied in a variety of forms. Today's motor cars are often designed this way. A basic design can, for example, be customized – that is, fitted with a variety of engines, or with extras like a sun roof or electric windows. This enables the manufacturer to offer a range of vehicles from the family saloon to a sporty, top-of-the-range special, all based on the same basic design.

Similar methods of offering customers variety are used with furniture. 'Mixing and matching' offers customers a way of building up a room setting to suit their individual requirements. Fitted furniture can be supplied in a variety of styles to fit in with different surroundings.

QUESTIONS

● Think of some other products where variety is obtained by additions to a 'basic' design.

● Suggest some reasons why people like customized cars or other customized products.

Designer choice

Customizing products to give them a personal touch has become a part of mass marketing (see page 27). But some designers go further than this. They have decided that they can often sell their ideas more effectively by sidestepping major manufacturers. Instead, they set up their own design and manufacturing concerns.

Although small when compared with mainstream marketing, this approach can be very successful, particularly with items such as furniture, textiles, clothing, jewellery, and fashion accessories. Designers can sell their wares direct to the public, at open-air markets such as Covent Garden in London.

Mary Quant's Bazaar in the Kings Road, London, 1966

Pop furniture, 1960s

Covent Garden, London: selling individualized designs today

Giving customers choice

Goods produced and marketed like this can sometimes be more expensive than mass produced items. But they can provide larger manufacturers with some competition, and thus help to boost the quality of design. Customers may often be prepared to pay more for an individual and distinctive piece of furniture or item of jewellery. This approach can also help designers to break through to wider markets, going on to become successful innovators in areas of design such as fashion.

QUESTIONS

● The alternative approach mentioned here has been successful when the consumers are younger people. Why is this, do you think?

● Why might it be difficult for designers to persuade manufacturers to take up new ideas?

It is always useful to be able to get good advice, and although manufacturers will happily tell you about their products, an independent source of advice can help consumers get an unbiased view. Interestingly, the **Utility scheme**, which was set up by the government during World War II, was a step towards this. The scheme was a vital part of the war effort, because it economized on the materials and production used for anything not needed to help fight the war. But it was also pioneering in that it laid down standards of design, materials, and construction for furniture and other goods.

Following this, in 1951, the British Standards Institute set up the Consumer Advisory Council, later renamed the National Consumers Council (NCC). This included people from manufacturing and retailing, together with journalists, teachers, and representatives from organizations such as the Women's Institute. The NCC published a regular *Shoppers' Guide*, which reported on a range of domestic products and indicated value for money.

The launch of *Which?* magazine

The success of this prompted the launching in 1957 of *Which?*, a magazine which aimed to provide plain, no-nonsense guides on the reliability, safety, and efficiency of many everyday products such as electric kettles, irons, and washing machines. The Consumers Association, which publishes *Which?* magazine, is independent of industry and is funded by subscriptions from its members, who in return receive monthly copies of *Which?*

Parliament also has a part to play in protecting consumers' interests. Acts passed by Parliament, such as the Consumer Protection Act of 1986, aim to ensure that the consumer gets a fair deal from manufacturers.

The Utility mark

Utility furniture, 1940s

Cover of *Which?*, 1958

Belling Type 852F	£19	1	8
This was wall-mounted. All others stand on floor.			
Ekco Thermovent	16	10	11
Ferranti CF6180	10	10	5
Morphy-Richards QR20	10	0	8
This had one 1kW radiant element and one 1kW convector			
Revo F14984	9	7	0

Above: Belling Type 852F (left), Ekco Thermovent (right)
Below: (from left to right) Ferranti CF6180, Morphy-Richards QR20, Revo F14984

Products surveyed in an early edition of *Which?*

QUESTIONS

● Why is it important for consumers to have independent sources of advice on products?

● Why was the Utility label useful to customers?

Consumer advice

Designing for needs

Today's technology is helping designers to meet many kinds of need – for example, those of the elderly and the handicapped. Many everyday activities which most people take for granted can be difficult or impossible for others.

In the home

Opening cans, operating switches, reaching high shelves, and getting up and down stairs are some examples of everyday problems at home. But designers can help disabled people in the home. Computer-controlled systems can be activated by very small movements, such as eye movements, and set to operate TV sets, telephones, or typewriters. These systems can even open and close doors, or switch household appliances on and off.

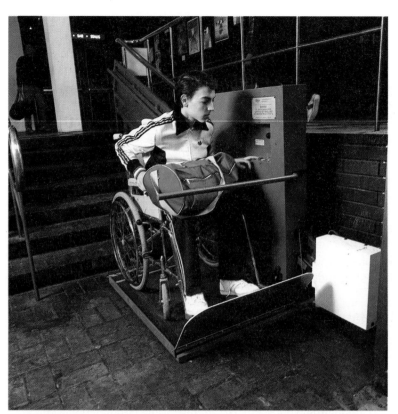

Chair lifts can give disabled people access to the different levels within buildings

A simple safety device helps pour boiling water from a kettle

This device helps arthritis sufferers to open jars

In the community

Designers are also becoming more involved with the needs of handicapped people in the community. Local authorities are now required by law to ensure that handicapped people can use libraries, museums, and other public buildings. Electronically operated doors, ramps, and lifts can all help to make life easier for people in wheelchairs.

Thoughtful design can help to ease situations for those who have a physical handicap, and so enable them to take a full part both in the home and in the community.

POINT OF INTEREST

Britain has an ageing population. Some 18 per cent of the population are now aged 65 or over, compared to just over 6 per cent in 1911.

QUESTIONS

● The pictures on these pages show some problems faced by handicapped people in the community. Make a list of all the others you can think of.

● When you are out shopping, try making a note of any features which are designed to assist handicapped people.

ASSIGNMENTS

● It is always useful for people to be able to get sound advice on consumer products. Design a consumers' broadsheet which could be published in your school once a term (perhaps as part of your school magazine), and contains information on local good buys that would be of interest and use to the people in your school.

Get the help of your friends to gather the information, and also to find out the kinds of thing people would like to have included.

Design promotion

There have been a number of attempts over the years to promote greater awareness of design. For example, the Great Exhibition of 1851 (see pages 22–3) was intended to serve as a kind of showcase for designers and manufacturers. Since then, other exhibitions have included Britain Can Make It (BCMI), held in 1946, and the Festival of Britain, held in 1951. Both were important in different ways.

The BCMI exhibition came just after the end of World War II, at a time when both industry and the public needed a boost. Although over 1300 products were on display, very few of these were available in the shops – as some people said at the time, Britain might be able to make it, but Britain couldn't have it! But BCMI succeeded in its broad aim of making the public more aware of the work of designers.

The Festival of Britain was held to mark the centenary of the 1851 exhibition, and promoted not only British product design, but also some of the latest ideas in technology, architecture, and urban design. There was also an air of zany optimism – and a hint that design could be fun as well as 'good taste'.

Festival of Britain, 1951

The Design Centre

A permanent display of products was mounted at the Design Centre, which opened in London in 1956. All the items on display were selected by the Council of Industrial Design (now called the **Design Council**). The displayed items were given the Design Centre Award. This became much sought after among designers and manufacturers as a kind of certificate of design worthiness. The Design Council is government funded and is independent of any manufacturing or commercial interests. It holds regular exhibitions, and takes a particular interest in the work of young designers.

Ideal Home Exhibition at Earls Court, London

Since the 1950s, design promotion has also taken other popular forms. The Ideal Home Exhibition, held annually at Earls Court in London, promotes the latest designs of domestic products. In addition, there is today a vast range of magazines dealing with just about every kind of consumer product, from cars to video cameras.

QUESTIONS
● Why have people involved in design thought it important to promote design awareness among the public?

What is good design?

From the heyday of the Arts and Crafts designers early this century (see page 9) right through to the work of the Design Council today (see opposite), the kind of design promotion we have just looked at has stressed qualities such as fitness for purpose, soundness of construction, safety, and reliability.

Some artefacts do indeed seem to bring these qualities to life, creating a standard which finds a permanent place in the public imagination. Some of these classics of design are generally acknowledged as masterpieces of the designer's art. The William Morris chair (see page 9) and the Wells Coates radio (see page 12) are among these.

Some design classics. Suggest reasons for their lasting popularity

Differing ideas on good design

Other artefacts seem to have won public affection through a special charm which has grown out of popular acclaim. An example might be the Volkswagen Beetle or even the famous Coca-Cola bottle. The world of fashion has tended to emphasize style and image as important ingredients of good design. Here, the emphasis is on constant change, with a continuous search for the new and original – out with the old, and in with the new!

Some people might claim that judgements about what is good design are purely personal and subjective. Looking, as we have been doing, at design in its social context, we need not be too surprised at these different ideas on what is good design. People have different needs and interests. Society changes through time to produce new ideas and generate new needs and new attitudes. These differing needs and changing attitudes are bound to be reflected in design.

Volkswagen 'Beetle': a cult object?

QUESTIONS

● Are there qualities which all good design should have? What qualities would you include?

● What turns an ordinary artefact into a cult object?

Designing for diversity

Product design today covers an ever increasing range of goods. This is partly because of progress in design and manufacture, but it is also because today's consumer needs are more diverse.

Children, young people, the family, the elderly – all represent different groups of consumers. Each of these groups has different needs, different interests, and varying amounts to spend. In a society such as ours, many people have a growing amount of leisure time, more money to spend, and are living longer, healthier lives.

In addition, the way we dress, the furniture and appliances we buy, and the cars we drive all tend to some extent to be an expression of our own individual personality. This, of course, is as it should be. It would be a dull world indeed if we were all the same!

Thanks to modern design, everyday life today is easier

When all these things are taken into account, we should not be surprised at the ever increasing diversity of needs, interests, and attitudes we find. And of course, we would expect to find this diversity reflected in an ever increasing range of products that people buy.

Is design today dull?

But does this diversity lead to a healthy diversity in design? Some people fear that although we are now better off, mass production of goods can lead to uniformity, and stifle creativity in design.

QUESTIONS

● Make a note of any products you think could be improved by more creative designing. What kinds of improvement would you introduce?

Pop music: creative or just commercial?

The accelerating pace of technological change has made us more conscious of the fact that we all live in one world, a world with limited resources. Yet people have many different needs, and some of these may conflict with others. We need energy to power our cities, to light and heat our homes. But this need can threaten natural resources.

Scientists warn of the danger of the greenhouse effect, caused by burning coal and oil, or of damage to the ozone layer (which protects us from harmful ultraviolet radiation) caused by chemicals found in some aerosol sprays and fridge cooling systems.

Our oceans may be in danger from pollution by poisonous wastes dumped as industrial by-products, and the loss of the world's rain forests may be a serious threat to the climatic balance of the whole world. We need to balance our needs against such dangers.

Designers share responsibility

Designers must share responsibility for the causes of many of these problems. Many of the products they design are made from natural materials such as wood and metals, which can be hard or impossible to replace. The products themselves – cars, for example – may burn fuel, which contributes to air pollution and also to the greenhouse effect. Packaging, the spin-off from advertising and marketing design, can also waste precious natural resources, and create environmental hazards. **Recycling** used materials is one way to preserve resources.

QUESTIONS

● Make a list of products you think may be harmful to the environment.

● What kinds of damage do these products cause?

ASSIGNMENTS

● Litter is a problem. Choose a part of your local environment (school fields, local park etc) and make a study of its 'litter cycle'. Devise a scheme or series of measures to improve the situation. This may include education and publicity campaigns, advertising, sponsorship, local council involvement, recycling and proper disposal.

Power stations supply energy, but can be a source of serious pollution

Destruction of the rain forests

Some of the packaging we throw away each day

Conflicting needs

Design with responsibility

Designers can use their influence in many ways to overcome threats to the environment and the waste of resources. Together with manufacturers they can:

■ avoid the wasteful use of natural materials;

■ use synthetic substitutes (such as plastics) where this causes less damage;

■ use recycled materials where possible;

■ use **biodegradable** plastics for packaging where possible;

■ develop designs for vehicles which continue to improve fuel efficiency;

■ design vehicles to run on other forms of energy;

■ design products to last longer, and to save energy.

This list could be much longer, of course. But it gives some idea of the ways in which designers might use their skills to reduce waste of materials and energy, and reduce the threat to the environment.

Biodegradable and recycled packaging can help reduce pollution and waste

Improving design

Many designers and manufacturers are working to achieve these objectives now. Some vehicles are already designed to run on gases such as propane, which is less harmful to the environment. The electric car is another possibility being explored, particularly for town driving, where its introduction would help reduce pollution and cut down on traffic noise. Many everyday household items such as detergents, polishes, and cleansers are being sold in more environmentally friendly packages made from recycled materials, or from biodegradable plastic.

The careful redesign of household appliances can also bring benefits. The jug kettle shown here is energy saving, since it can boil smaller quantities of water. It is made from tough plastic with good thermal efficiency, which also helps save energy, as well as being less likely to burn anyone who accidentally touches it while it is hot.

Prototype all-electric car

QUESTIONS

● What other ways might designers use their skills in to make the environment safer?

● Take a household appliance (for example, a hairdryer) and suggest improvements that might be made to its design.

In a rapidly changing world, designers have to face up to their responsibilities. But responsible design can also be fun.

The pumping station shown here is built on the Isle of Dogs. It houses sophisticated pumping machinery which is ready to come into action if the River Thames threatens to flood the surrounding area. By careful and colourful use of materials the architect has created a building that looks interesting. The architectural forms used have echoes of the past, while at the same time symbolizing today's technology in an exciting way. The massive columns look like parts of a fortress, but they also function as ventilation shafts.

Pumping station on the Isle of Dogs, London, 1988

New ideas for everyday artefacts

Product design can be exciting too. The designers of the torch shown here have given the product a new image and have improved the design at the same time. The switch mechanism is incorporated into the retractable handle. A lens bulb assists focusing. The beam can be angled by tilting the top. Raising the side casing switches on a second bulb.

The torch can be hand-held, carried by the retractable handle, or stood on a flat surface, leaving the hands free. The tough casing feels good and projects a distinctive high-tech image.

Durabeam torch

QUESTIONS

● Take an everyday artefact and see how many suggestions you can make to improve it by careful redesigning.

Note: it took two years to design the Durabeam torch!

Finding new forms

The challenge to design

Designers in today's world have to cope with designing for a great variety of needs, many of which may be in conflict. The task that they face is an increasingly difficult one. Designers will need to exercise their skills and use their influence even more carefully and responsibly in the future.

Technology will continue to evolve and people's needs and interests will doubtless change. Yet this offers all those who work in the many different branches of design some exciting challenges. Important among these will be the development of more energy-efficient products for both home and transport, as well as more environmentally friendly products.

Looking to the future

Increasing leisure will give designers and manufacturers opportunities, particularly in areas such as clothing, sportswear, and fashion. Consumer electronics will continue to grow, with designers seeking new forms for products such as videophones and pocket phones.

As consumers we too face the challenge of coping with an increasingly sophisticated world in which an ever greater variety of products will compete for attention. We will need to become more design aware, so that we can be better equipped to make sensible decisions about our purchases.

But there are encouraging signs. People, particularly those in younger age groups on whom the burden of the future mainly lies, are showing an increasing flair for style and individuality, together with a more critical attitude towards consumerism. The future is looking good!

QUESTIONS

● Make a list of what you think are the most important challenges facing designers today, and explain why they are important.

● Make a list of the ways in which people can become more design aware.

Some of these products may be available in the near future

Glossary

Architect Someone who specializes in the design of buildings.

Artefact An object designed and made by someone.

Arts and Crafts Movement A design movement led by William Morris, in the nineteenth and early twentieth centuries.

Biodegradable Capable of being broken down by bacteria.

Celluloid An early form of plastic, made from nitrocellulose, camphor, and alcohol.

Civil engineer Someone who designs roads, bridges, tunnels etc.

Consumerism The sale and consumption of all forms of goods in modern Western societies.

Design Council An independent organization set up in 1956 to encourage higher standards of industrial design.

Division of labour Method of manufacture introduced in the eighteenth century, in which workers specialize in one part of the production process.

Gothic A style of European architecture popular from the twelfth to the sixteenth centuries, used most notably in churches and cathedrals, but much copied in the eighteenth and nineteenth centuries for other buildings.

High-rise Tall buildings, such as offices and flats, which are constructed with steel framing and concrete.

Mass production System pioneered by Henry Ford, who used standardized parts and a moving assembly line to speed up production.

Modernism A design movement concerned mainly with architecture; started around 1920, led by architects Le Corbusier and Mies van der Rohe.

National Census A survey conducted every ten years by the government to discover trends in the size, distribution, and make-up of the population.

National Parks Areas of natural beauty set aside as parks by the National Parks Commission, established in 1949.

New towns Towns established shortly after World War II by the government to take overspill population, mainly from large cities such as London.

Nylon A synthetic plastic invented and developed in America during the 1930s. The first nylon stockings were sold in 1940.

Packaging The materials (plastics, cardboard, glass) in which many of today's products, in particular food, are marketed.

Parkesine An early form of plastic, invented by Alexander Parkes during the 1860s.

Planner An expert in planning the layout of towns and cities.

Plastic A general name for a wide range of materials, mostly synthesized from petrochemicals, and used for a vast range of products.

Polythene A synthetic plastic developed in Germany during the 1950s; used for containers such as bottles and buckets, and also for piping.

Recycling The processes involved in recovering materials such as paper, glass, and metals for re-use.

Ribbon development Housing, mostly 1930s, which extended along roads leading into towns and cities.

Standardization Making components to a standard pattern or design.

Utility scheme Scheme laying down standards of design, materials, and construction, mainly for furniture and clothing; started by the government during World War II.